D1003040

Pacifists in Bomber Jackets:
Cartoons by Isabella Bannerman
© 1998 by Isabella Bannerman

For information contact
Roz Warren, Laugh Lines Press
P.O. Box 259, Bala Cynwyd, PA 19004
email: rozwarren@aol.com

Printed in U.S.A.
Cover art by Isabella Bannerman
Cover design by Ellen Orleans

Library of Congress Catalog Card Number

97-074489

Pacifists in Bomber Jackets:
Cartoons by Isabella Bannerman

p.   cm

ISBN 1-889594-04-0

1. Humor

I. Isabella Bannerman

Pacifists in BOMBER JACKETS

cartoons by

Isabella Bannerman

■■■■■■■■■■

for

Jimmie

■■■■■■■■■■

Keep Your Marriage Interesting:

SARAH AND HER ALL-DAY MUFFIN

Same Address, 20 Years Later...

DIANE REMOVES HER LOVE BEADS
BEFORE RESUMING TAKEOVER NEGOTIATIONS.

IF YOU EXPERIENCE EYE STRAIN AT WORK, SIMPLY FOCUS MOMENTARILY ON SOMETHING FAR AWAY.

THE AILING MATISSE TRIES CUTTING OUT
MEAT AND DAIRY PRODUCTS.

Lester, the Lazy Dentist.

Karen deciding how to spend
her evening.

PUNK RAPUNZEL

21

What you might find on the dinner plate...

in New England,

and in New York.

BANNERMAN ©13

GEORGE'S SPECIAL CREDIT CARD GAVE HIM
ENTRY TO MANY WONDERFUL PLACES.

As a matter of fact I am an artist,
but I only draw blood.

SCIENTISTS FIND PROOF THAT MEN REALLY ARE FROM MARS:

Oh no— not another Philips head.

MICHELLE'S BUREAU OF ALCOHOL,
TOBACCO AND FIREARMS.

Conversation for a Small Planet:

HOW ANIMALS MARK THEIR TERRITORY.

LAWYERS BOARDING A PLANE.

Domestic Beers

It's the rug you've been sweeping things
under that gets pulled out from under you.

Archaeologist finds the first food pyramid.

After dinner, the women retired to the
library to discuss old boyfriends.

It's time to move out
when Mom says,

STUDIES SHOW THAT...

Women talk ... facing each other,

Men talk ... side by side,

and that Men _and_ Women tend to talk simultaneously while gesturing wildly *

*Researchers do not agree on who starts the yelling.

YOU TRY TO CHANGE TV CHANNELS
WITH THE CORDLESS PHONE.

Romance in Swampland

Household water use:

VIVIAN HOLDS A QUICK MEETING.

WOMEN TRADING PICK-UP LINES

HOW TO: FLATTEN YOUR TUMMY!

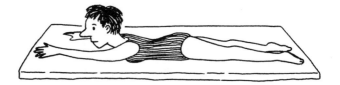

Lie face down on the floor.
Your tummy will flatten.
(Added bonus: You can do this one
by the pool, at home, or any-
where else people usually lie
face down!)

BANNERMAN©

A child of the 60's,

and her little daughter, Backlash.

56

ACTUAL EXTENT OF DOUG'S OFF-ROAD ADVENTURES.
(SEE BOX FOR DETAIL)

SEE SPOT GET AROMATHERAPY.

Why do Old Hippies Smile?

FEMALE STREETSMARTS

EAST:

CONCEAL
EVERY-
THING
BUT
THE
EYES

WEST:

REVEAL
EVERYTHING
BUT
THE
EYES*

(*AS LONG
AS YOU
CAN
MOVE
QUICKLY)

BANNERMAN©

KEN'S BACK WAS BENT
AT A RAKISH ANGLE.

FLOWERS THAT SAY TOO MUCH.

EXISTENTIAL TRUCKSTOP

DUBIOUS ADULT SUPERPOWERS

ROGER WAS ALWAYS DELIGHTED TO FIND NEW CLOTHES
JUST LIKE THE ONES HE ALREADY HAD.

Follow Your Bliss...

and the bills will follow.

REALIST TRAC: WITH 4 SETTINGS

1. BEING LATE FOR WORK
2. DOING LAUNDRY
3. CARRYING GROCERIES
4. RUNNING FROM MUGGER

BANNERMAN © 6/96

WHEN THINGS ARE SLOW.

The Brave, the Proud, the Cold:

The Women Who Won't Wear Hats.

PERHAPS SALLIE HAD MADE HER
BOOKSHOP TOO COMFORTABLE.

TAKE ME TO YOUR THIGH MASTER.

Finally. A home exercise system that really is a clothes rack!

Mismatched Mantras

ONCE AGAIN, JOEL GOES FOR HIS
SECRET 'HOT-APPLE-PIE' OPTION
INSTEAD OF CASH.

PROGRESS OF A BOOKSHELF

URBAN RELAXATION

CAREER TRACK MEETS MOMMY TRACK
ON A NARROW SIDEWALK:

GETTING READY TO HAVE FUN.

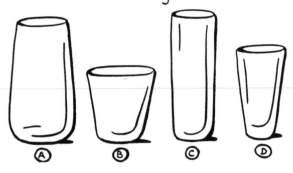

TEST YOUR SOPHISTICATION!

Can you match each glass to the correct beverage?

1. Instant Breakfast drink __
2. Powdered Laxative __
3. Diet Milk Shake __
4. Vitamin Supplement Formula __

BANNERMAN © '64

Entymologists in Love

LAUGH LINES PRESS

publishes a full selection
of cartoon and humor books.

To receive a free catalog,
please write:

Laugh Lines Press
Post Office Box 259
Bala Cynwyd, PA 19004

or e-mail RozWarren@aol.com